Cusp

Elaine Briggs

Cinnamon Press
:: small miracles from distinctive voices ::

Published by Cinnamon Press
www.cinnamonpress.com

ISBN 978-1-78864-173-9

British Library Cataloguing in Publication Data. A CIP record for this book can be obtained from the British Library.

Designed and typeset in Bodoni by Cinnamon Press. Cover design by Adam Craig © Adam Craig.

Cinnamon Press is represented by Inpress.

Acknowledgements

I give thanks to the editors of *Envoi* and the *Poetry Salzburg Review* in which some poems first appeared. 'The Head' was placed second in the Hungry Hill Poets Meet Politics competition in 2016.

The warmest of thanks go to Jan Fortune for her energy, care and consideration in editing this book.

I am similarly grateful to poet friends Joc and Gordon Simms, erstwhile organisers of the Segora competitions, whose encouragement never falters, and Anne Morgan, who introduced me to the surprise of Wallace Stevens' poetry; to Rachel Boast and Jane Monson who advised me along the way; to the wonderful Geraldine Green whose writing workshops 'On the Farm' supplied nourishment when required, as did our visits to the quiet pews of Cartmel Priory; and to Robin Thomas, the best of mentors, whose keen ear and calm maieutics saw some of these poems develop into their current selves.

I would also like to express gratitude to Peter Briggs for supporting my decision to take early retirement in order to be able to devote my time to writing; to my daughters and granddaughter for their affectionate interest in what goes on their grand/mother's head. And lastly, my admiration for two women, Annette Huguet and Sylvie Rault-Maisonneuve, who showed me that not only was the door not locked but that it stood wide open.

Elaine Briggs has lived in France for fifty years, and has French and British nationalities. She worked as a professeur agrégée in middle schools, lycées and university, teaching students English language and literature. Alongside this work, she was also a translator specialising in contemporary art – work that she continues to do today. She took early retirement from teaching in order to devote herself to writing. Her poetry has won, been placed or short-listed in various competitions including Hungry Hill, Segora, Cinnamon. Individual poems have been anthologised by Hungry Hill, Segora, Forward, and published in Envoi and the Poetry Salzburg Review. Work has also been read at the Theatre by the Lake, Keswick. She is an avid consumer of KDrama. She has three daughters and one granddaughter.

Contents

Then I felt like some watcher of the skies

                                    Keats

Fully then appeared the moon

                                    Sappho

Cusp

Afterbirth

Aren't we all born
from the sea
the amniotic ocean
already full
of broken promises and
crash-landing futures
sight not yet
awakening the caul
beneath the eyelid
still amnesiac
the strung-out body
barely pre-pubescent
surfing on the tail
gate of the cargo plane
taking off
pale youth compressing
time and space
in that poor apology
for a rib cage
hauled on board
full face into
the leaden desert red
sunset amnion and chorion
shredded to flakelets
by toy taketombos.

The Egg Bearers

My daughter, keeper of chickens,
gave me eggs, one with two yolks.
I cracked it open, scrambled them.

Was the laying hen the wild one?
When the feed seed is scattered,
she attacks, beak thrusting.

There are never enough cartons so
the eggs go in a paper bag,
shells risking the trip.

Daughters, granddaughters
with their supplies sitting tight,
hold their paper bags of love and memory.

I would un-menopause my love,
crack into memories, pre-poached,
slipped into ziplocks, waiting.

Child

how did she know
as a child she would within
bluebell and pimpernel
gazing observing
knowing why
they were they
knowing the innerness
of bluebell blue
pimpernel red
smooth lanceolate
tiny heart
sad droop
placid smile
a world peopled
with growth
the facts of colour
and texture
even stones spoke
as they held her hand

Anna's Hummingbird

if only the adults saw the answers
to the hard questions are simple

a broad world
a light cover of tree and sky over

a childbird who's never learned
to walk, only fly

and how tiny the nest
scribbled with scraps of lichen

swaddled in spider silk
is all   if not

only a glossy bolt of pink
then nothing

The Veal Calves

they approach like shadows
breathe out vapour, sun-transparent
no expectation in their dazed eyes

some chew the cud, the only sound
that disturbs our gaze waiting at the gate
for the slow tread of the white calves

The Ides of July

On coming to my first garden of France it also was enclosed,
a simple paradise fenced in and, marked out,
veg beds, dirt raised up a little
from the beaten earth paths,
ways empty and borders full.
We ate all of it, even the twitchy rabbit
with the round eye one Sunday in its hutch.

The mother working the plot wore fine blue ropes
under the tanned skin of her arms
and rope-soled shoes, black was her favourite
colour though she was not a widow.
She forgot to advise me to close
the window at night so in bed I got bitten asleep
at some weird hour when the owl stopped,
his ears having strolled out of their shells
to catch the nightjars now despite themselves
slipped back into their deep dark recess.

The daughters' names were not a problem,
she made them motherly clothes and cut their hair
like boys, cropped. The kitchen was not
their daily domain either. Her name was
an embarrassment, neither Maman nor Madame
but the dull old grandma was definitely Mémé,
she made overalls and tablecloths, covers.

The mother took us to a pop concert where we saw
Dalida, famed for the coquetterie in her eye, sing.
I had no idea who she was. We also went
to the beach and ate baguette
with dark chocolate. Without an alibi,
between two disappearances, the husband,
an engineer, came too. He watched the length
of my legs, my diffuse midriff. I was glad
for a flat chest and that I had no tongue in my head.
The savage pinch in writing came only much later.

Rape

Bare of leaves and shade,
her canopy has capsized
every fault in the earth's skin.

Bark split by heartwood gaze,
a sap-swollen headtie hides
the delayed blade-twist within.

Stuff

there's stuff that guilt and fear will not say,
stuff hidden from the glare of the sun,
under rotten logs, nesting woodlice, unstill, in a clutch

an instinctive glimpse suppressed of the child
too soon hand-fed into mourning,
young student standing hopeful,

hitching a lift, then seated,
a blank before the camera lens,
the click and lock of the shutter held fast

Sea Smash and Pearl

Are these ungracious lines of clay part of her DNA,
did they make up her original being, a recreation of
what she was. It's not as if she's been put back
together with liquid scars of gold, broken

in Japan and her fragments beautified to be more
than a woman—Aphrodite wind-blown in twists and turns,
folds and recesses, abscondita on learning Zeus
never fathered her, only sea smash and pearl.

All these tests for the sake of authenticity. To know
that the score written for her was a tone lower,
not the flute but the oboe.

What is this other? A single sperm brazenly
laying claim to half of her. And suddenly all
lineaments and likenesses have a new reading.

Blood Clot

In the nose, mouth, mind—smells
from the long-ago reach
of a greenhouse.
Dried blood to feed
never-quite-ripe long arms
of green grapes, green leaves
ripped off to relieve the shade.
Other blood seeping upward
from the rows of cats (a joke?
skinned first? chopped?)
buried below, trespassers
killed each with a blow from a clod
of earth to the head.
More dried blood, specks
on a fresh shaved chin,
styptic pen, tear of toilet roll
stuck on, Axe lotion coverall.
Fiction blood spattering the
kitchen wall ketchup-style.
It leaches everywhere, feeding
on life's staples, inheritance,
patterns of lineage, patents
of paternity.
            Like rain,
blood is silent, its only sound
a rebound when hitting the something
to which all flow is bound.
Three score years or so
later, there is a wish
to have no name,
no one should have a name,
like the gods, we would be absent
from ourselves, the veiled familiars
of shadows and dreams,
contour free, lineament free,
neither contained in veins
nor container.

Stone Time

three of us out
walking one winter
the road a straight light rise

the girl tall thirteen
body outgrowing mind
drags far behind
then flashes by in a spurt

mother presses down
on her stick on my arm

she wants to take me
—I think it's too far—

past the low grey expanse
the estuary of salt and mud

the standing waste the flood
clumped with grass like straw

then, lodged in a flake of slate
we see it, a skeleton bird's foot
embedded fossilized gleaming

an imprint
in the timed-out sun

Mother floats over the Kent estuary to Grange and all points west

Bay window over an estuary, mist lowering
and a roll of water shrinking to a pale stripe.
A shallow bridge straddles the scape. Squat piles
compress distance and a short train floats

over, slippage in thin air. Of this, she sees
nothing, living in wasted memory, in gaps
thickened with cataracts, windows
full of themselves. Her mission:

body rocking, soothing reeling
humours. Clad, fed, laved by
fleeting figures, hushed, still
questioning this side of the hard glass.

When I left her for the last time, I would have
stayed a while quiet in the car, looked
over the estuary. If the tide was in,
I would have admired the broad expanse,

grey, uncluttered, and remembered
the speed with which it charges up and ebbs away.
If it were out, I may have thought fearfully
of the monks guiding travellers over the safe path

avoiding quicksand. If in the admiring frame,
I would have let her glide along the viaduct,
prow to the front carriage. At the Grange stop
she would descend and take a turn along the Prom,

droplets of well-being misting annuals and perennials.
She would sit and wonder if the faint horizon vertical
was Blackpool Tower where, in the twenties,
she took tea with the maiden aunts, the bad lad uncle.
I would be sure it was not.

Mother, you were never native here, tone-deaf
to the faults and gorges, the granite crags. So, a truce—
let us ignore the tang and stings of nature,

let's gather speed in flight, as if together
we'll leave behind the final curlew's human voice
and at the last, breathe open sea air.

Holy Saturday

Far away above the sea, a heat haze
clinging to the edge of the world. But, on the ferry,
visibility is perfect, optimal distance of clarity.

Just made it to the port. If only she had known
the way timed to an end does not much matter,
rather the scenes off to the side, probably
a bright sapling-filled slope over the murk of a failed river.
She barely spares them a look hurtling down the A road,
concentration going to pieces, jolting to hold the course,
stamping on the brakes, no consideration, reliving
the tremor of sparrow bones crushed under a wheel,
blind flight flushed into the path of heedless intent,
the leering Friday night drunk trapped unconscious
and thence into waiting shadow
            passer mortuus est
when to either side of her was a safe passage,
a cradled settlement, a barn.
But then, she never had her children's backs.
What should she expect when she fails
to tend her own back garden, silver grass bent and broken,
clematis run wild over walls designed to keep her at bay.

Stashed among clumps of sea kale on golden expanses of pebble,
distanced stragglers sit still on the strand, winter-pale isolates,
and her heart beats ever slower in greeting to the yellowing dog,
fangs bared, no visible injury, drying out on the kerb at Oxford.

Trinity

after The Virgin and Child with Saint Anne, Leonardo da Vinci

Statistically commoner, mother's
mother sits on rocky heights in a
gaze of melting protectress;

mother, awkwardly balanced in her
lap, tips out to the infant errant,
sacrifice for all harm done.

Now we have graduated to that mythic three,
will the bloody stain of ancestry cease to leach?
Good question since the future's nowhere to be seen.

Knowing the father is often a gamble. He
tends to dance away under veils. Maybe
he's holed up in those mountains vague

to the rear, off-white snowfalls mired
through to misty slush, shaking himself off,
loose-muscled, heavy-bodied, insubstantial.

Onlooker grandmum, me, unable
to speak knowledge, enabled the trouble.

In our case, three fathers in a row
going missing is a bit of a joke.
A lesson in unknowing teaching

how to draw a blank, the zero before
presence and before less than nothing.
That vital number safeguarding balance.

In reply to Daughter who Messengered me when I was not online

I live isolate on a rim in this urban hermitage,
mind wandering empty free through forests, down rivers,

ears tuning in to the dull roar of night
or the magic of fingertip music by day.

Unless a promise has been made, I am all unawareness, unfit
for the fluster of response, echo, conversation.

So why this sorrow that I missed your call,
this apprehension of the dawn bird's mockery.

To All Our Specialists: Peace, Good Fortune and Wellbeing

As is our annual wont, we book the appointment.
Gold and silver change hands, symbolic for the
verdict, the edict, the prediction.

We quaver. She lurks. Straggly snakehair, as per usual,
embroidered robe usual, the raving, roving eyeball
usual, bellrattle usual.

She shakes, prances, trances. Jinglings scrape
our tympanum, our fovea. She divines our womb,
radiates our joints.

Brainwaves tingle, breasts flatten, epiderm freezeburns,
arteries catapult. Our gurneyed being lies helpless. Does she
need birds in flight, patterned

offal on a tray? When will the augury fall? She speaks:
I am retiring soon, next month.

The Tap

The new chrome bathroom tap
sometimes looks like a one-eared rabbit
sometimes a sea-horse with flared nostrils
as if it doesn't know
if it would run hot or
if it would run cold.

The minds of taps are like this
especially late at night
when shutters are shut
and the bed doesn't beckon yet
and there is a sadness in the mild pit of the belly
at the idea of running whichever way.

Of Bathrooms and Sarcophagi

Is it only the naked drops of water
or the idea of the daily cleanse
that brings you, fully fleshed, into view?

And must you always bring her,
silent as a tomb, expressionless,
along with you, invading my white-tiled zone?

You stand as a unit some way beyond,
allowing me to turn around you,
much as I did the celestial couple

reclining together on their sarcophagus,
high cheeks smiling before the eternal feast.
Moulded in a single piece of clay,

they were sliced in two through the middle,
so as to survive the heat of the kiln.
The woman's feet are daintily shod for heaven.

The Head

Part of the face is substantial.
The right nostril is present,

as the left eye, the mouth,
and the balance of the face.

The right eye, most of the brow,
and both ears are missing.

The most arresting feature
is the left eye: wide open,

it is formed by a raised line.
The lid's curvature is delicate.

Full-lipped, the mouth shows
a philtrum that is well-defined.

By the corners are drill holes.
A fine indenting of muscle

is left over the upper lip.
Softness permits a satin

finish with crisp detail.
No trace of the hair.

Folds of flesh overlap
where were the cheeks.

The prominent chin
presents a marked knob.

Major damage indicates
the head was smashed expressly.

The Green Bowl and the Concubine

Quiet, on the cusp, in readiness,
the bowl sits awaiting repair since
it slipped from the hand
and neatly broke.

It looked lovely,
strange, a long curve down
and a vertical rising to the rim,

white calligraphy manifest,
ready for a hand to close it and
make it whole.

In fact, the break was so clean
that the bowl could make a semblance
of unbrokenness and sit quiet attending
the royal decoction, on the cusp.

Gold Seam

Eyes reviewing the flowers proud
on a spray see depths of red,
paler coral and how a twig might branch
over a petal, the brush of a line

obliterate a cupped cluster,
the dark stamen dots and what of
the single bud that lay apart,
afloat on the pale green ceramic.

A memory of that kind was needed to survive
the dead thud as the painted jar slid and broke
exposing inner whiteness, sparkling crystal
sugar. No flowers ever held within.

Decoupling

I

Tethered, staring ahead
as if to a window,
our full-length portrait
awaited completion.

    In an instant of frozen abandon,
    a snapshot offered itself.
    Tongue held, you turned away,
    a collage of back, neck, head.
    My eyes sifted drifts of sand
    for a hand or face.

Visitations fell away,
dipped along the ocean's edge,
folded, unfolded the lullaby.

    Houses lining the shore lay in ruins,
    coats of mud tilted boats.
    Returning from the sea,
    prying stone from a wall,
    ochre and grey, I grazed a knuckle.

Exhaustion knows neither ruins nor boat,
stertorous breath jerks me awake.
If only words on dry paper made barricades,
or razing thought yielded the solitude
with which my heart could fall in love,
errant knight around its bed.

    Your body once lay alongside mine
    and I would have covered it with my worn one
    had other hopes not cleansed my touch from your mind.

II

One colour will suffice.
Defeated hearts have no desire
for electric daubs in tranquil graveyards.
Sunsets appeal to the past,
it alone colours them red.
Let thin grisaille paint
the mistiness of today.

> Grainy grey, no moon,
> mauve dusk dimming
> the towers on the silent plain.
> Skeleton pylons, once we landscaped the sky.

No compass, no sundial
will forecast, beyond sight,
life's shadowy indigo.
Anguish lies in the fixity
of the future, not the past.

> Whitecap bubbles burst,
> and absence, that watery notion,
> is hard to apprehend. Foot by foot,
> the falls' silky lip pulls the canoe.
> Stop before the clear skin goes over the edge,
> wade out in the greywater rush,
> see the splash cloud make a rainbow arc!

The ablution is enchantment.
Eddies and spray cool the eyes,
mist skin, heart, mind.
Spellbound words ooze
vapour, unintelligible.
Then, skim and slip over marble
breast and hip
sluice of chill
icy sting
the need to know
why desire exults
why summer heat spins to thunder.

The words and I force quit our shady recess.
We plot an exodus, imagine odes,
bud an extravagance of plumes.
All leads back to the theoretical desk,
the window in suspension, dust and motes
floating between pen and page.

Inosculation

after William Harvey's The Circulation of the Blood, 1628

By some initial planting did this occur:
two happy seeds dropt by birds in flight,
one winged sycamore, blackthorn one.
We grew together, knowing no other,
touching, rubbing, enlacing, and as
we swayed in the wind's artful play,
thus our surfaces abraded away
and through veins and arteries inbled
braided our limbs became. But,
all things are not alike so easily attracted
or repelled. Had our subtle mouths stayed
in like manner continually closed, no process
could ever contrivance have found
to pry them apart and light would never
have been allured. Yet those searching
instruments being in us dilated, some little
of the other's fluid did drift within, and then,
in the manner of a tide or Euripus, poured
in mutual motion back and forth.

Nature it was instituted those membranes
through which our cambia came
into play, for it was never ordained
that our heart be stressed with needless
labour, either to bring that which
had been better kept away, or to take
aught that needed to be brought.
Therefore, contiguity came to both,
to both belonging, so that
both be more copiously supplied
with nutriment so pure and simple
as coming immediately from our heart
than from our brain's disingenuous folds,
or our lustreful eyes, or indeed our flesh.

Pavane pour enfants défunts

for P. S.

We did not know what
we had, you and I,

a love too precocious
even to be amazed

teenage discovery, let
alone understanding.

Our love was unsafe
but we did it nonetheless.

Decades pass, and
I think of you again,

an afterthought,
like your initials,

wishing you were
here to swathe me.

We should have met
later in less fluid

a world, one in which
ignorance would not

have led to miscarried
blood of life being

lost forever.
That road not taken,

did our failed infants
gain paradise?

It's Alright, That's Love

On the white road
the full-grown man stands
at the three-went way.
To his right
sudden low shifts
inhabit the soft waves
of rice-green growth,
to his left
the future glade of saplings
straighten at the side
of arrow bamboos.
A culvert ducks away.

He stands full of tears,
eyes never unsealed,
bare feet scarred
with dried blood,
an undelivered teen
like a four-year-old,
a wounded leveret
limping away with his mother,
one shoe on,
one shoe off.
The red tin-roofed house in flames
the ash of dead,
a scattering of neighbourly houses
silent in a valley of green.

Worlds Apart

Or you as cartoonery,
irresistibly mindless,
an obituary picture
ready-framed in black.

On the screen, how to
stretch a line into life
— oofle-dust pigment
and magic sparkle pen?

Moving images having writ,
pixels lie dead,
lines ghost and smear,
though plasma and glob can hang

still in a frame-freeze crash
spill, and body fluids span
random from droplets to
vapour splayed artfully in arcs.

Graphics give endless space
to move through your liquid
crystal blood and think of
you as inked-out final splash.

If love were to straddle our worlds,
would it ordain more stills,
fewer special effects, redact
the ready-made bubble script?

Egret and Coypu

Up by Chambord, the Loire seems to lighten,
no bridge to shrink it, no island to divide it.

We picnicked perched on awkward branches,
baguette raggedly torn apart, cheese squashed on.
Bubbled in our own amusement, we nearly failed to see
the hare's thunderbolt scud past our feet.
But the fright made us live to the place.

Five egrets fished in a line along the sandbank.
Evenly spaced, a team, they trawled subaqueous gleams,
and when the murderous crows arrived overhead,
two sheared off to mob the party-crashers.
Then they took their line dance higher upstream.

Clear sandbank, clear sky. The coypu stuck up a head, periscopic,
waggled its flab and stringy tail over the beach
shooting droplets in a porcupine spray. Flop bask snooze.
You have that talent: wait, dance your shadowy steps, circle slow,
you know how to suspend a kiss.

But what of the thrill of entering the river's band of wild intent,
seeking the break of sun on water from below?

Encounter

We chanced on this parapet in another world,
you're fast away and I'm fixing the horizon.

You asked me to fetch your shoe before you slipped
into sleep and it fell twenty feet below our station,
one high heel of a pair of cloud-grey slingbacks.

Your head rests on my lucky shoulder,
it's a gift for me, everything is now a given,
the coordinates are plotted, the line to be conducted,
lightness of air and I'm no longer drunk.

On the mortal path we chose, I saw the vanishing
point blazing with a pin-prick of light
forging us back to innocence.

How many sleeps will you sound before
you scissor dawn and walk toward me?

You

after the poems of Jeong Ho Sung

Don't cry in that place. Fluorescent
lights are too harsh for gentle tears.

You longed to be far away, listening
to petals murmuring, falling,

and before you knew it, your path
was flooded with flowers.

No sound of a river flowing,
ring of a cellphone calling.

From now on, I'll have no memories.
When I fall dead drunk in the alley,

I'll still task you with lighting the night.
I'll come to you even when you don't.

All winter long, you'll silver
my heart with snail tracks.

You'll deal with daybreak too,
just like the moon.

We

A path doesn't easily find
a way,
strong winds ruffle its surface
flow upstream,
force time back, and when
the visitor
on the path comes to you,
body's casket full
of past, present and even
future, it may
already have been broken,
the heart,
so I say to yours that today
is always
the first time meeting the tremendous
expanse of ocean,
seeing each ripple overflow
one other one
making its way for the first time,
and I am scared too.

Lubh

Oh, the sedimenting layers we tread down,
heavy-footed, unaware.

You were perfect. Stendhal's branch
thrown down the salt mines at Salzburg.

You emerged—or I withdrew you?—
dripping white with crystallized diamonds.

I had nothing but clichés for you: you
made the stars eat out their stone-dead hearts.

But I wanted you imperfect, here and now
giving me twiglets of heart-untwining lines.

Right to left, left to right, your cool
turns of prose complicated debate.

None of you was love, just a measure
of loneliness from our pasts.

O.E. *lufu*, O.H.G. *luba*, L. *lubet* (*libet*)
lubido (*libido*), Skr. *lubh*: to desire etc.

Oh, oh, the layers of fine ground salt
in this gradual etymology of love.

Secret Affair

Mozart, Rondo, A minor
I play this for you
and start my day

it says this is life
come rain or shine,
it whispers to look
after grief and to love

Mozart, Rondo, A minor
I touch these notes for you
and start our day

in half-step ascent,
we expand the air
our hovering voice
the lark's sad song

Mozart, Rondo, A minor
I hear your touch
and start my day

turns unfold
contour resolves
in rhythm serene
counterpoint

Mozart, Rondo, A minor
you know this dyad of keys
my touch starting your days

quieted, legato we span
a melodic refrain
a procession of chords
orbiting yearning

Mozart, Rondo, A minor
so few notes
to play the wisdom of a day

Orpheus, Tinnitus

I dreamed Eurydice
nested in the redness
of a cochlea.

Her eyes held the measure of the world.

A fine metal skewer from ear to ear,
her strident cry,
pierced my drum.

It hurts just a little
when I make my song

Weave Unweave

My door is a bramble, its loom a tapestry
where I sit, tailor made, above silken prickle threads
and blindly weave a matted mess with interlocks
of leaf cane root, and still it admits the night foxes,
their bright eyes that eat the glistery clusterberries,
the darkling drupelets, and spore all the seeds
beyond my tentered warp and weft, out past the grasp
of my tight-grouped skeins, their exotic spectra,
their cinnabar wings and smooth-oiled ink
sloshed senseless by that skank of a fox-tailed brush.

High on my loom, all I can do is grip firm
to the brocade's govern, the narrow floral border
treadle-thumped through folding paths of cloth
spilling oh so lightly through liver heart lungs,
through sing of fingers and pluck of toes,
but my eyes, those loons, ramble off to the lake,
it inflects my gaze, and they sigh so bad for a glitter fix,
the needle prick of pixels shed by dust of moon.

Vapour

More clouds have come and gone
than I can tell, droplets gathering
in their own way, dissipating the same …

much as I do with vaguery
to haze my face, then a melt,
small water for the garden plot.

Born but not begotten, no truth
came my way knitting and stitching,
raggedy threads catching, hangnail hem.

Parking de nuages, so spake the child
timing our meetings and passings,
poetry making itself in future rain,

placing her faith in the westerlies
as if to gentle us in sleep and dream,
mackerel rippling cold atoms up to the stars.

Woman with Rose and Ice in Bottle

after Wallace Stevens

Must rose not bloom in ice,
neither in the mind
nor in reality,
its petals only a little despondent

in their war with the cold
moonlight night,
only a little scentless
by delusive temperature.

A rose in bloom has no fury,
nor the heart of the matted
thorn twigs. No idea
that ice is an aberration,

no notion that creation's
wintry warring daughter
is the destroyer.
Rather that bloom and freeze

were never moon-crossed
loves, that old tropes,
rose and ice, can realize
thought, content the eyes.

Still Life

Nature Morte au Chaudron de Cuivre, Chardin, Musée Cognacq Jay

the copper pan
done by Chardin
not a real one

not in the sun
gleaming
reflection

lifting sheen
to matter

and back
all alone

The Translator and His Harp Sing the Iliad

A harp is a made thing,
the heartwood of Homer, an ode.

It's a flightless wing
with speech in its keys

and strings taut and resonant,
open for winds to frisk at sea.

It's the prow of a boat
where Orpheus turned helmsman

set a rhythm
for oars to dip and rise

and the water that streamed from their blade
outsang the Sirens' wolfish howl.

You stand alone, your frame
spindly as the African lyre you cradle.

Then, in an Afghan cap worn for a crown,
you swell—wind and breath

sing to me the Muse's song and
the rage is re-made of Achilles.

Not St. Valentine's

6th January 2021

I am seated here quietly bookish
in my favoured option: non-invasive retreat.

Shapeless wool is my drab for dream,
I do not black robe up like Machiavel
entering his studiolo as if it were court.

But what option in the command and control
holding sway over booklessness.

What of those who stormed the Capitol,
did they give thought to their dress
before dishing out death as if no end to jest.

It is no small fortune that pianists need only
a push-button behest for disruptive chord
attacks to play into my fingertips.

Violets

Just now, looking for a poem
to share, for thee and me to read
together, I came across one on
violets, yellow or blue big blue,

not the deep purple or white now
in flower, placid powder scent
too low for me to kiss, sweet
woodland must. The page held

a bookmark with a photograph
of a young man's torso naked with
diamanté crucifix and it made me
think of that actor so I had to

smack it verso blank to stop thinking
of poets in Paterson and wanting
to cry. I betook myself to Iamus,
babe forsaken on a bed of violets.

Cute fact: he became his father's
priestly interpreter of birdsong.

Viewless Wings

By the Stream, a Chill on the Air
See, poor heart, how the upended bee angers the flow,
spinning-top wings buzz-fight the stream,
or, scarce aware of grace, sun-filter branches tingle the river
and its dull, tinned skin, sensing surprise,
starts to speak in bubbles.

Will our lowly stretch of dirt-water now sparkle laughter?
Will it get caught out in an eructation of belief in life?
Or will our every -oid and -osis,
gall on the bark and shiny green chafer in the rose,
rod and ring our lacklustre straggle, our horsehair self-pity,
back to the old single track of what once was
and is no more, not so much chosen as blithely followed
for being less milkily faint in the early mists of spring.

November is upon us and no prelude yet composed,
nor has our mind, let alone you, heart, conceived.

Slow Draught
How small wine slippers the throat, alder finger-roots
dipping into bland painlessness, the lenifying
melancholia once reported to school the soul.

Little drowning difference,
in the cool of belated age,
how deep, how often one drinks.

Exodos
The sad bird's song is long gone that nameless bird
I never heard though once I chanced on
a rossignol pouring its soul
to an alien world.

I returned there time on time, watched
it lend my voice to dead of air, through indigo
press of night unroll my speechless heart from vineyards'
corn-row braids to improbable expanse and undecipherable sky.

Heat

Swans have fled to the one surviving lake,
cut off from river trickle at Saint Genouph,
who once gave fight to *le mal des ardents*.

Body movement, through a hollow
perhaps at the base of a hedge,
may persist mycelial, barely a tickle.

Opposite banks are estranged, a still, a haze.
Thoughts powder in cavities, too much insulation
against wet, none against dry and hot.

Extreme—term with no quench of warmth,
no lover's attentive ear—shrouds to itself
all registers, voids the steady flow that knew
at once our rhythms, verses, cadences.

Strange to Relate

The banana leaf unfurled
between yesterday and today.

At first, a rolled green brolly
or edible scroll, now already
hooding over

like its siblings, minus
their wind-torn shag.
It can still do a back flip,

it's not the full downward arc yet,
the fronded broken flap. Shame
it's useless bringing forth

still finger fruits, unable to ripen,
and not decorative,
yet my eyes are drawn to it,

so full of elsewhere.
Unlike other leaves and needles,
a branch in itself.

And here's the neighbour's cat come
to view me through the window.

Myth

The night's message
is a glimmer tide-ruffle
of white and dark.

Then comes the phosphorescence,
seaweed on volcano sand.

Stars implode.
Others bawl the nursery drama of birth.

Most will join the filamentous conga,
billion upon billion of years round and round
in Hera's breastmilk.

When he asked me if
I was a mermaid, I lied
there were no mermaids
except in children's tales.
I asked him if he was from the stars. To which
he lied there were no stars, only gas compressed
to matter. The waves, as usual, were busy
recombining futures, it's what they do.
No questions asked. Though all our children will say
As I lay in my cradle, I wiped a tear.

Paradise

When grey dawn damp
coats the nape of your neck

and I stroke a thousand flowers
around your throat,

you fill my nostrils
till by dint of inhaling

musk we are rendered odourless.
Jasmine does not last a day.

We prune the laurels,
unkink the veins in the leaves,

fork open a life
in the beds.

Our knife-edge garden is all
a balance of deadhead and bud.

Guardian

Released from the dead of morning,
gaps in the shutter observe
the blue cedar, and it me.

It sighs and stirs
lumps in my throat,
small candle cones

dropping into a spongy mush
for the kids on bikes
to practise their skid turns.

Atlas sits jovial
on the big top, doesn't want
to shoulder a tree roots up.

Heron

sun strong wind strong
blue sky hard from edge to edge

stand of poplar stresses in heat
dry gold crackles underfoot

bees amok in mint-scented air
small lake lip-laps at mad ripples

outrageous squawk and heron
lifts into shadow flight overhead

broad Vlad flap with impaling beak
lands in stubbled field-span

evolutionary argument for pterodactyl stasis
isolate statue eying the competition

cellphone lens clicks time into place
and the earthed bird is airborne

riding heavy   scouring folds
of hilltop plains water bound

Sand

That morning the sky drew on day, opening
over the oblong garden bruise-orange.
Its heavy unfamiliarity was somehow bland,
unarresting, a blank-out of different hue,

leaving clouds blind and deserted in a loss
of identity—no rush of wind or lazy motet,
no spangle, no flotilla parade, no relation
of particularity to wash of uniform blue.

Two mornings later, the heavens sieved
themselves free of sirocco sand, and we
were left amazed—how the desert invaded

our realm, coated the honeysuckle and sage
we felt were our gifts to grow, behold and love,
as if eyes had been sleep-filled for an age.

Villandry

I

Love in sight

April 2nd, Palm Sunday

Sky low, Jardin du Soleil fenced off.
Vines pruned, topiary chess pawns
tweaked, limes pollarded as if cankered,
but buds teeming on the knobs say not.

Glimpse of red tulip tip. Contained.
Chinese honeymooners play tag,
rush together, hug, kiss.

Outside the walls, strimmers buzz.
On the quarter hour, the church bell pings
and birds twit. What mystery in the art of canon-ing!
A daffodil nods and sinks, arms outstretched. Pietà.

The wood, haze in the hand, lists beyond reach.
The giggling lovers are embraced in the maze.
The heart of it found with ease.

II

Shed and shred

early April

The human hand is there everywhere:
the clumping pollard stumps,

the lawnmower stripes,
the gravel rivulets,

the topiary, the humanized
measure, the lineated baby

lettuce, the wave of brunnera blues—
so much that the dandelion obtrudes.

And what of us, our offcasts,
hair, nail, skin, cloth,

the DNA stamp.
Me and the Chinese lovers,

we blend our intimacies,
our viewless portraits,

even as we pick up grit
in our trainers.

III

Shade, or not

mid-April … et les fontaines sont en eau!

The Sun Garden is open and its god
not long past a zenith, playing shadows
with pollard fists, hornbeam tracery.

Tulips point skyward, not yet
the gape-mouthed abandonment
of loosened petals.

I am enjoying my ten minutes
of skin cooking, pores titillated
open and glad to be swan still

in the silvery grass blades,
the lovers' lilt, the warming stones,
the girl's cartwheel plus back flip.

Birdsfoot Trefoil

Minute in your lakeside camp
of rough dry grass,
I can barely make you out.

Imagination makes up
what the failing eyes
and the ramrod backbone

cannot grasp. That blur
of yellow, I think, divides
into swollen claws tipped

with orange fire, spurring out
from plain clover-like leaves.
Thus, a brief account of you.

Because the wonder of knowing,
carnally as it were, getting under
the whys and wherefores of

your vanilla scent, is superseded
by faint memories of you,
and bluebell, pimpernel, speedwell,

days when you gemmed small worlds
of childish delights, long days when
essence of pebble would hold a hand.

The Song of the Black Geranium

between there and here, the black geranium
has come inside out of the cold into the warm

in truth it isn't black though sometimes it seems so
as snow isn't cold, under-layering heat

down to the roots of everything, and sunlight
through glass has gingered it into flower

in keeping with the black that is in fact
carmine which sounds like a song

Stalk Flowers

Months of absence still inhabit
the back garden, dank plumes

of grass, misborn seeds stilled
in a fug of cloud, rotting

in birdsong's loony slurs. So why
remember a moment in the greenhouse,

your fingertips pressing geranium leaves,
offering me their apple-green zest?

Shortest Day

no fixed form as yet
a mix of lengths at a slant

rainfall rods dark and silver
naturally blending the drench

birds' gonad blast
craving sweet life

contagion in the urge for a word
a snowdrop uprooted in the green

Pelargonium 'Dark Secret' on the sill in January

The deafness of nature's obstinate fertility,
the squabble as small brown birds' gonads swell.

In their tiny mind, nothing more than length
of day's actuality magnifying stubbornness,
soon to be nesting under a bramble tangle roof.

Meaning no more or less than the necessity
of being, somewhere in world's stream and time.

Not meteoric, nor metaphoric, no lessening
because they have no words whose one joy is
to span the gap, even when spoken out of turn.

An unsettling effect, the darkness of the red,
the stamen pricks of saffron orange, almost
too much for flowers to crow in the weak sun.

Journey

Pushing back branching vegetation,
a glass of night wine teeters unconducted,

rests at length in a sway of canopy,
surveys the stars littering valleys

rivers plains folds. New moon arcs
sharply. Why would drunken words want

to play. Where is the point? And yet
is anything like this, so lonely and lovely.

Forest Ride

The forest ride makes a couple of turns
downhill to an outcome sealed in leaf and mystery.

Closer, butterflies vie over heads of knapweed,
asphodel runs to seed, and here

bark is lifting off trunks, crusting keratoses
slumped into a mess of needles and grass,

the low voices unheard in undergrowth. Far and near
are nothing to pine winds that bemoan no home.

Moon Low

In this river city, I car cruise along the banks,
ageing wanderer, opening and shutting

screens, whose vistas of beauty I often fail
to see—an iris's flagrant blue in February,

bird flurry on the feeder—so intent am I
on fallen tears in a study stupid with books

seeking the etymology of all aching things,
I nearly missed the huge moon low in my face.

Pool at Giverny

ears half in easeful love
with a limpid trickle

notes plucked
from a virginal's cords

thoughts in a warm pool
flagged in yellow and shade

sun filters alder
through peaty water

waxed from the depths
light submerges pale

shafts of earth in suspension
a brush laid down oil and pigment

electric touches in pink and blue
reach greedy from the deepest past

Maulévrier, Jardin Oriental

forget the glock
of bamboo on bamboo
forget the sun streak

coursing over the catalpa
timing indented bark
forget the strobe on water

forget the cursor
rippling expectation
forget the curl of carp

don't look deep
see the pond skater
jerk into a feat of movement

viridian lake spume
is there for you
to walk on water

The garden waits in the scent of lilies

I

Intent of matter, growth and decay,
eludes stewardship—
the lilies serve the bees, the beetles.

A stormy electric night to come,
anther powder washed away.
No matter, so few bees.

Only a moment for
loss of smell to turn to grief.

II

Knowing the roses' season is over,
the lilies secretly rise through air
on stalks quivered with many tongues
and silently radiate their love.

A downpour blast, the sky blots out,
insects scramble under, away.

The sky re-opens, the lilies keep their quiet.

Notes

Holy Saturday: *'passer mortuus est'*: from a poem by Catullus, 'passer mortuus est meae puellae' (my lover's sparrow is dead).

Of Bathrooms and Sarcophagi: 'the couple reclining together on their sarcophagus': Etruscan terracotta sarcophagus known as 'of the married couple', Cerveteri, c. 520 B.C., now displayed in the Villa Giulia, Rome.

The Head: based on 'A Fragmentary Egyptian Head from Heliopolis', Jack A. Josephson, The Institute of Fine Arts, New York University, The Metropolitan Museum Journal.

Viewless Wings: 'viewless wings', 'alien corn' are from Keats 'Ode to a Nightingale'; 'school the soul' is from Keats, a letter to his brother.

Heat, *'Le mal des ardents'*, or ergotism, aka St Anthony's fire, a form of poisoning after ingesting a fungus that infects rye in particular, and in the Middle Ages thought to be the Devil's work.

www.ingramcontent.com/pod-product-compliance
Ingram Content Group UK Ltd.
Pitfield, Milton Keynes, MK11 3LW, UK
UKHW040437280225
455666UK00003B/139